The Fragile and the Fierce

Poetic Remedies for the Tender,
the Tired, and the Unyielding

Angi Sullins

POEMS

THE RED TENT BLANKET FORT	7
THE FRAGILE AND THE FIERCE	9
FRAGILE FIERCE BELONGING	11
GRIN	15
WONDER LIKE ARMOR	17
STAND SPEAK RESIST	21
THE STONY RIVER	25
TENDER FIERCE CREATURES	27
THE WINDOW	31
THE PRICE TAG	35
THE PIÑATA MAKES A COMEBACK	37
A BETTER ENDING	39
STAY	41
LIT	43
THE COMPLIMENT	45
THE VILLAIN	49
WISHBONE	51
THE KNIFE IN THE STORY	53
JAWBONE OF FORGIVENESS	57
PRIDE	61
THE SECOND FIRE	63
ARC	65
THE REACH	67
THE COST OF FORGETTING	69
FAITH	73
THE ACHE THAT KNOWS YOUR NAME	77
A LETTER FOR EEYORE	79
WINGS	81
STORYTELLER	83
STAY IN YOUR STARLIGHT	85

BRILLIANTLY BAD	87
THE WAY	89
A SPELL FOR WHEN YOU FEEL LIKE LEAVING	91
FRACTURE	95
STILL	97
PROMISES KEPT	101
DAFFODILS AND STARDUST	105
BIGGER ON THE INSIDE	109
RAINBOW	111
THE POP QUIZ	113
WHY REJECTION IS RAD	115
THE SHACKLES	117
BLACK SHEEP GOSPEL	119
WHAT IT MEANS TO FLY	123
THE WHIP	125
JUICY MESSY GORGEOUS	127
THE RIDE	129
JULY	131
TRUE WEALTH	135
WAR PAINT	137
ORIGAMI IMAGINATION	139
FERAL HOPE	141
JANUARY	143
MAMA BEAR	145
SHARK TEETH	149
MORE	151
SPARKLE	153
TACOS	157
THE LANTERN BEHIND YOUR RIBS	159

© Angi Sullins 2025. All rights reserved.
www.AngiSullins.com

No part of this publication may be reproduced or transmitted in any form or by any means, electronic or mechanical, including photocopy, recording, or any information storage and retrieval system now known or to be invented, without permission in writing from the author, except by a reviewer who wishes to quote brief passages in connection with a review written for inclusion in a magazine, newspaper, broadcast, or for publication on the Internet.

Cover design © Silas Toball 2025

ISBN: 979-8-9994319-1-2

Published by Duirwaigh Studios www.Duirwaigh.com
Printed in Canada.

This book is dedicated to my fellow empaths, misfits, and love warriors who strive to keep their hope and strength alive in a world determined to crush them. It's ok if all you can manage to do today is feed the dog, pet the cat and eat some soup. I believe in you.
Now go brush your teeth.
I love you.

THE RED TENT BLANKET FORT

come in love
wipe your feet on the mat
made of past lives and poetry

this is the place
where the weary
and the weird
finally exhale

the red tent blanket fort
is pitched in the heart of rebellion
stitched with threads
of remembering
and lined with silken hope
it hums like a lullaby
and growls like a gryphon

this is no ordinary fort
this is a reclamation
filled with quilted courage
stuffed animals who've seen wars
and hand-stitched spells
woven from velvet and vengeance

misfit?
me too
too much?
you bet
too loud?
good—we have
pillows for screaming
and our tree neighbors don't mind

too tender?
we have tea and tissues
and a wolfpack of empaths
who'll hold your hand
while you remember your magic

this is your haven of heathens
your temple of trustfall
your sanctuary
made from second chances
and midnight snacks

we celebrate
crying at pet videos
and stampeding like bison
when the world tries to hush us

here
you don't have to choose
between softness and strength
you get both
because our tenderness is a blade
and our snuggles are strategy

this is fierce rebellion
in flannel pajamas
anarchy in fuzzy socks
a revolution
wrapped in satin and sass

so come in kindred soul
curl up with us
under a roof of stories and stars
you don't have to be anything
but exactly who you are
welcome home
you belonged here
before you ever knew
this place existed

THE FRAGILE AND THE FIERCE

they told me
you can't be the storm
and the flower
choose they said
be soft
or be strong
never both

so I broke their rules
and grew
thorns on my petals

some days I cry
over broken feathers
other days I break
the rules that broke me
both days I am powerful

they never taught us
that being tender
is its own kind
of rebellion
that letting yourself
be seen while you're still
shaking
is bravery in bloom
that the hands folded
while saying grace
carry claws
like promises kept

I am the quiet
and the scream
the prayer
and the battle cry
the open hand
and the sworded fist

the truth is
I am not either/or
I am both/and
I am the fragile
and the fierce
a song
of my own making

FRAGILE FIERCE BELONGING

sometimes exhaustion and activism
sit side by side
sometimes they play footsie
under the table
while enjoying a pot of fondue

sometimes
anger and compassion square dance
spin your partner do-si-do
at a honky tonk joint
outside of town

reverence and irreverence
have been known
to give piggyback rides
to each other
the two of them snort-laughing
their way down the aisles
of All That's Holy

the sacred and the profane
are next door neighbors
they serve sage truffles
and strawberry boxed wine
at their Thursday night book club

the foolish is my saucy friend
and the wise my midnight lover

this means I can march
in the streets with a bullhorn
a human torch of rage and compassion
then
curl into the shape of grief
in a fort made of hope blankets
then
cry feathered tears for
the tiny broken robin's egg
on my driveway
and still use words
like dicktard and cuntwaffle

two things can be true
at the same time
like this poem that seems
to rhythm and rhyme

and then doesn't

let this be your
get outta jail card
when you hold yourself prisoner
inside the smallest simplest
version of you
the cleanest you
the compliant you
the chameleon you
no longer needs to conform
to the one-crayon picture someone else
colored you to be

stop demanding the world be
one thing only
or expecting people to comply
with your version of sanctity

life itself is a juicy
contradiction
a hot glorious mess
of entangled beauty

so are you

live it all
let it all
then own it all

authenticity is sexy
accountability is the new pretty
transparency is the little black dress
that can take you anywhere

get real
and then wear that realness
to every event
it's the spicy accessory
that goes with everything

this way lies the zip code
of your genius
where your deep joy
feeds the world's hunger

this way lies
fragile fierce belonging
as it sways
with reality
to a jukebox lullaby
on a floor of sawdust and wonder

GRIN

they told me
to smile more
so I sharpened my teeth
and grinned

they told me
to make myself smaller
so I grew wings
and took up the whole sky

they said
*you'll never survive
without us*
so I learned to build
my own fire
and howl
under my own moon

they call it rebellion
I call it remembering

remembering that my voice
is not a sin
that my body
is not a battleground
that my soul
was never theirs
to tame

resistance
doesn't always look like
shouting
sometimes it looks like
choosing yourself
over and over again
without fear guilt or shame

they wanted my silence
I gave them my song

WONDER LIKE ARMOR

in the burning times
people will tell you to harden
build walls
not wings
the world is collapsing
don't you know?

but she
she painted her eyelids
with stardust
and walked barefoot
into the rebellion

she wore wonder like armor
the delicate kind
that marvels
at hummingbird flight
the moon's night blush
the mystery of a spider web
and the geometry of a nautilus

the kind of wonder
that survives by keeping vigil
for the child heart
in every human
and the ancient kind
forged from the lullabies
your grandmothers whispered
while the bombs fell
the kind braided into the hair of witches
who hummed against the stake

the kind of wonder
that's survived every apocalypse
by growing wildflowers
in the ash

they thought it was foolish
her ruby-throated joy
her circus-colored courage
her refusal to bow
before the god of despair
but what they didn't see
was how many wars
she'd endured
just to keep the light on
in the window of her soul

wonder was never her escape
it was her shield
her banner
her bloodline

while the world ravaged
she sang

while men in suits
crowned themselves god
she dreamed and dared

when the elite separated
the worthy and unworthy
she wove stories
of beauty and remembrance
pouring whispered awe
into the broken places

she went to bed each night
with the ugly and atrocious
scratching at her door
and tucked wonder
under her pillow
so she'd wake each morning
determined
to love the world anew
not because
she didn't see the fire
but because she was the fire
and wonder
was how she danced
inside the flames

STAND SPEAK RESIST

stand
not because it is easy
but because it is sacred
because your spine
was forged
in the phoenix fire
of every woman
who came before you

you are the descendant
of witches who refused to burn
queens who ruled barefoot
with crows in their hair
and wild girls who carved poems
into the bark of the world
so they would never be forgotten

speak
because silence
is a false language
forced upon your native tongue

they taught you to whisper
but your soul came here
to sing
to roar
to dance truth
over the spine
of the earth

resist
the story that says
you must be small
to be loved
your grandmother's goddess
was a woman who ate
mountains for breakfast

and picked her teeth
with the bones of trees

unbind your hunger
uncage your joy
shake your hips into galaxies

expand
because you are
not here to fit in
you are here to awaken
to light lanterns
in the minds of sleeping stars

you are not a rebellion
you are the return
of something holy
so when they try
to unmake you
with doubt
with shame
with fear
remember

you were formed
of comets and coronas
of rune storm and battle cry
you do not owe them
your silence
you owe the world
your fire

speak my love—
chant wail
spill scream
tell shout declare
sing
like a goddess
who finally remembers
her true name
is a song

THE STONY RIVER

grief didn't knock
she kicked the door down
and made herself a home
inside my chest

I asked her how long
she planned to stay
she laughed and said
I live here now

she sits next to me
at every dinner
never eats
only watches
she steals my sleep
borrows my breath
shrouds my heart
in locks made
of rusted tears
hides my laughter
like a lost key
I'll never
find again

some days she's a whisper
a whimper
a wail
other days
she's a wrecking ball ghost
in a wedding dress
white
haunted
beautiful
destructive

I try to fold her
into poems
into prayer
into petals
but she refuses
to become
anything but ache

people say
it gets better
what they mean is
you get better
at carrying the grief
without spilling it
all over the room

what they mean is
you learn to share your pillow
with a home invader
and maybe spoon
on nights when
the moon is too full
for words
and tears become your
mother tongue

grief is not
a wound
you wait to close
she's a stony river
you learn to cross
every single day

barefoot
brave
bleeding

and still
I walk

TENDER FIERCE CREATURES

"You're so brave and quiet I forget you are suffering."
—ERNEST HEMINGWAY

When someone calls you strong it can sound like a compliment but feel like a curse. I've been called a trooper. A powerhouse. A champ. One family member refers to me as a spiritual Timex. (Remember those ads? *Takes a licking and keeps on ticking.*) I'm so persistently encouraging of bravery, chance-taking and wonder hunting that people don't hear the sniffles, the long sighs, the jagged ugly cries. They think I live a charmed life, moving from happiness to happiness, success to success.

So wrong.

Even though I share regularly online and in person about my vulnerability, anxiety and struggles with suffering, that part of me is often overlooked or misunderstood. It's quieter than all the daring adventure, but it's there. And when I do share, people often consider me a lighthouse. I'm the resilient one. The capable one who chooses to focus on the light. Just because someone runs a bold race doesn't mean they don't walk long acres of doubt.

When one chooses bravery, it doesn't mean they don't struggle with fear, anxiety, overwhelm. Intense self-reliance and resilience can be the painful result of emotional abandonment or neglect. When no one ever shows up to help or support, nurture or relieve, one must make a choice what to become. I became a lighthouse.

I cry easily and readily in front of people, though if you are the cause of my hurt, I'll likely downplay it so as not to make you feel bad. I'm no longer proud of this. No longer think of my ability to mask pain as a badge of honor. It's a trauma response. Most certainly learned early as a means of keeping myself valuable to the few people raising me—especially because they did not share their tears, though some could easily share their anger with a belt or a paddle.

This silent shame claimed me early.

I'm five years old. My pet rabbit Bun Bun has died. I sneak off to my room. Even with the door shut, I don't feel safe to cry. I open the closet door and bury myself back behind the dresses and coats. There, in the pitch-black darkness, the sleeves of my favorite sweater catch my tears and muffle my sobs.

It's my 15th birthday. Friends have gathered. There's a pink cake with frosty roses. A surprise guest—a girl I haven't seen in years—comes into the living room and we both squeal and run to hug each other. Her shoulder snags my pinky fingernail and bends it back until my flesh rips. The pain shrieks through me. I announce to the room, "I gotta pee" and rush to the bathroom to cry. Sob. The water running over my finger 'til there is no blood and no more blotchy proof on my face that I have been wounded.

I'm 19. It's mid-afternoon and the guy I'm dating is on my childhood bed. My parents aren't home. I'm still a virgin and as a recovering Baptist, very conservative about anything more than making out. When kissing turns to a blowjob, my first, I'm caught between wonder and terror. It's over so fast. There is no talking. There is no reach for me—towards exploration, or pleasure or release—to bring me to the same euphoric state that he's in. As the seconds tick by, I realize I've been seduced into a giveaway rather than a mutual exchange. I love this guy, so it hurts. Bad. I get up quietly, hiding my face because it's already leaking. I go to the bathroom and cry. I don't come out until all traces of my agony are invisible.

For most of my life, the dark closet has been the only safe place for my pain. If I've processed it and crossed over the shame sludge, I'll share openly, vulnerably, even publicly. But if the pain is real time, it's almost always silent, even with those closest to me. Only in recent years has that begun to shift, due to the deep dives I've made into trauma therapy and CPTSD study. Apprenticeship to the dark underbelly of childhood pain has allowed me to unwind the traumatic neural pathways that kept me in shame and silence during real-time suffering.

The relationship between lighthouse resilience and dark closet vulnerability? I call it the dragon butterfly effect.

There was this guy, years before my husband Silas, who flirted outrageously with me online and then invited me to a late lunch at a steakhouse outside of Atlanta. It was a stormy day. The thunder kept interrupting our conversation. He was a strapping fellow, biceps bigger than my beer mug. The dazzling smile and pretty-boy eyes told me he was used to getting what he wanted. I liked it though, because he was confident without being cocky. A rare find.

We enjoyed a flirty but deep, rich, philosophical, three-hour meal, which ended with him propositioning me to a hotel. "Oh no, sorry. Before I share my body, I need to share heart space first. Sex for me isn't a plaything. You're better off with others for that. At this point in my life, I want play accompanied by meaningful exchange, deep respect and mutual emotional investment."

He didn't take *no* easily. After my third refusal and his honest reply that he didn't want anything serious for now, he cocked his head and considered me quietly. A beat, two, three. "You're a conundrum. You're a dragon, all hot fire and ferocity. But inside, you're a butterfly. Tender, delicate, vulnerable. Not too many guys can deal with that."

"Then I'll wait for the one who can."

I drove down the rain-pelted highway thinking I'd avoided swallowing a jagged, bitter pill. I was proud of myself for not responding to his glorious and compelling charms. I'd learned a thing or two since paralysis, date rape and multiple mismatched dating heartaches.

As the windshield wipers swished the downpour *left right left,* I searched the brooding skies for wings, wondering how many creatures might be trying to make their way through the storm. And how many lightning-bolt women shelter a heart made of delicate wings.

No matter what you're going through, you are allowed to be both fierce and tender. Your dragon bravery is needed in this world, as we struggle to bring change to a fractured community. But your butterfly vulnerability is also necessary, as it allows us to recognize ourselves in the mirror of your fragility.

We are tender fragile creatures. When we experience shame, but dare to break silence, sharing imperfectly, we grow powerful wings and strong, capable teeth.

Both are necessary. Both belong. Don't let anyone tell you otherwise. Especially yourself.

THE WINDOW

dear girl who has survived,

I know what you're thinking
that joy is for people who haven't seen
what you've seen
that laughter is a sound
that belongs in other people's mouths

you've learned how to survive
on scraps and silence
you've built armor out of
just fine
and
don't worry about me

you've become a master
at pretending
and so when joy knocks
softly
like a hummingbird landing
on your windowsill
you don't know what to do with her
she is small and bright
and unfamiliar
you are scared
you might crush her
with all your ache

but let me tell you something
joy is not asking for permission
she doesn't need you to be unbroken
she is not here to erase the past

she is here to sit beside it
to light one candle
in the room where everything fell apart

joy is shrewd like that
she knows how to live in
hard places

joy is a tender animal
she does not come roaring in
like healing
she circles the wounded woman
who has learned to brace
for absence
to call silence a friend
to mistrust every flicker of light
in case it's just another
match blown out
by someone who promised to stay

joy is not loud
she will not fight your fear
she will not demand her space
at the table set for grief
but she will come
quiet as dusk
startling as a nightingale
singing on a battlefield

and you
you might not recognize her
you might mistake her for a trick
or a test
or something borrowed
you'll be punished for wanting

that's okay
you've lived through fire
you've walked barefoot
through rooms
filled with broken promises

of course you don't trust the sun

but you're stronger now
not because you're unbreakable
but because
you've broken
and rebuilt
and broken
and rebuilt
so many times
you've become
your own kind of magic

joy is your birthright
a rebellion
a secret the soul never forgets
even when the body does
and I want you to know
it is not naïve to feel joy
after all this
it is not foolish
to let it touch you

it is brave

to smile when the world
has tried to steal your softness
to let your guard down long enough
to feel the warmth of something
that might not last

that is holy

let joy sit beside your sorrow
let them hold hands
you do not have to choose
one or the other

the miracle is that your heart
still has room

love,
someone who knows
what it's like to be afraid
of the sun but still
crack the window anyway

THE PRICE TAG

you're counting the cost
what if you fall?
what if the world
doesn't catch you?

but love pie—
the price of not trying
is the slow death of your dreams
and the quiet smothering of your fire
that cost is a debt
that'll bury you alive

go on
take the leap
because the only bankruptcy
worth fearing
is the one where you lose
yourself

THE PIÑATA MAKES A COMEBACK

life has been dishing it out lately
like a moody chef
with too much salt in her soul
and not enough wine in her glass

so I propose a revolution
not with pitchforks or protests
(boring)
but with piñatas

yes
you heard me

we bring them back
not for birthday parties
but for breakdowns

string 'em up
in the middle of the office
the kitchen
the trauma ward of your heart
wherever the ache aches hardest
next we hand out glitter bats
to every woman who's ever
been told to be polite
when she wanted to scream

fill those rainbow beasts
with chocolate
sour gummies
tiny tequila bottles
and notes that say
you are still magic even in pieces

and then
we swing
we wail
we unleash
years of swallowed rage
and all the tears
we converted into people-pleasing
until it rains
sugar and paper and liberation
and we're laughing through our tears
with caramel candies stuck to our cheek
and a broken bat in our hand
saying
this
this is therapy
this is medicine
this is me
coming back to life
one wild whacking swing at a time

because sometimes
the path to healing
is paved with confetti

now pass the peanut butter cups
I've got more feelings to bash

healing is messy
but it tastes
so
damn
yummy

A BETTER ENDING

we all have one foot
in fable
and the other
in fracture

we sip champagne
with dragons
then cry ourselves
to sleep in bathtubs
full of unanswered prayers

we wear ballgowns
over bruises
tiaras made
from caution tape
and catharsis

in the morning
we braid our hair
with strands of gold and grief
by night
we hold court with ghosts
who taught us how to twirl
on broken promises

we laugh
with our mouths full of longing
we ache under moon song
we dare to dream
even as the tigers circle
our firelight

we are paper cranes
with tattered wings
and steel beaks
part spell
part scar
part stardust

this is how we survive:
by telling the truth
with beauty
by dancing
on the line
between ruin
and rebirth

we are the story
and the storm
we live another day
to write
a better ending

STAY

you're not healing
to better shoulder sorrow
this isn't some gladiator game
where your softness is forged
into a sharper sword
for the next battle

no

you are healing
so you can finally stop flinching
when joy knocks at the door
so you don't mistake
tenderness for a trap
or delight
for a dagger in disguise

you are healing
so your laugh
can fill a room
without apology
without scanning the corners
for what's waiting to break it

you are not
training your heart
to survive another war
you are teaching it
to dance again
barefoot
beneath moonlight
without watching the horizon
for incoming storms

you are healing
to taste strawberries
without bracing for poison
to touch skin
without needing a backup plan
to receive love
without rehearsing
your exit speech

love pie—
your healing
is not a blueprint
for battle armor
it is a spell
to grow gardens
from the scorched places

it is not so you
can endure more
it is so you can feel more
the shimmer
the sweetness
the small good things
that no longer need to scream
to be heard by your soul

you are healing
so joy can find you
unguarded

and stay

LIT

she is lit from
within they say

incandescent

as if she swallowed
the moon whole

it's not that she was
born under a myth
or raised by a star

it's just the hope
inside her chest
she refuses to extinguish

because once
long ago
she decided
to live like a
lighthouse

bearing the light
in unbearable times

THE COMPLIMENT

don't call me resilient
like it's a crown
I wanted to wear
don't paint me
in gold resurrection
and say
look how she rises
as if I'm a phoenix
by choice
not necessity

you praise my strength
like it grew wild and free
from power
not grief

but darling—
my resilience
was not a poem

it was a scream

it was duct tape
and deadlines
and trembling hands
on the wheel
and nights crying
on cold linoleum
while the world insisted
I was tough
and had it all together

it was smiling in rooms
where I was bleeding
it was laughing
so no one would ask
why my eyes looked like
they remembered the war

so no
resilience
isn't a compliment
it's a scar
you named beautiful
because you didn't want to look
at the wound

it's the armor
you admired
so you wouldn't have to ask
why I needed it

you say
you're so strong
I hear
you can take more
but what if I don't want to?
what if
my vulnerability
is more essential
than my ability
to take a hit?

what if feeling
my feelings
all the way down
is fierce reclamation
of my authentic self?
what if I want
a life that bares
the naked
inconvenient truth
in my teeth

not just the sword
in my smile?

what if I am
just as strong
in my grief
and tender overwhelm
as I am when I'm
carrying on
or
as you like to say
walking it off?

what if I'm tired
of compliments
that support hiding
the fractures and bruises
so you can be comfortable?

I refuse to be
a crime scene
cover-up

I refuse to
be complicit
in falsifying
my truth so
I can win your
esteem

like there's a trophy
for suffering
and a reward
for silence

no

I'd rather hear
how brave I am
to be real in a world
that benefits from
fakery

how courageous
I am to feel my fear
and still show up fully
shaking
and imperfect

that I am a badass
for wearing reckless joy
bigger
than my damage

now *that*
Mr. Patriarchy—
is a compliment

THE VILLAIN

be willing
to be the bad guy
in their story
if it means you finally
choose yourself

if it means you
stop shrinking
stop hustling
stop breaking
just to make them comfortable

they will call you selfish
they will call you cold
they will twist your story
until it doesn't recognize itself
in the mirror

but the truth is
you're not cold
you're just no longer
willing to burn
for everyone else's warmth

you're not selfish
you're learning to love yourself
enough to stop pouring
from an empty cup

they will write you off
they will paint you in shadows
but boundaries
cast their own light
and authenticity is a beacon

your glow is a lighthouse
empty of apologies
and the right ships
will find you

you will never be
the hero of everyone's story
and that's okay

be willing
to be the villain
in their story
if it means
you finally become
the hero of your own

WISHBONE

darling love pie—
you were not sent here
to decorate disappointment
with glitter
not meant to make
a home
in the waiting room
of someone else's *maybe*

you are not
a porcelain prayer
meant to be placed
gently
on someone's shelf
and only dusted
when convenient

no

you were born
howling
a tempest wrapped
in soft skin
with thunder in your throat
and wildfire
beneath your ribs

so why now
do you whisper your dreams
instead of shouting them
like holy rebellion?
why fold your wings
to fit into rooms
built for smaller
souls?

stop

pluck the wishbone
from your spine
like the lie that it is

let go
of the sweet ache
of *maybe*

replace it
with the roar
I am
I want
I will

your backbone
is a cathedral
stand up
like god lives there

no more tiptoeing
in your own life
no more silence
when your heart
wants a symphony
no more apologizing
for wanting
the entire sun

get up
gorgeous rebel
there is no cavalry
coming to the rescue
you are the hero
you've been waiting for
and that's a good thing
'cuz ferocity is its own reward
and it looks so damn good
on you

THE KNIFE IN THE STORY

you thought they were kin
you swore oaths under moonlight
shared salt
fire
secrets
you carried their grief
like a second skin

but one day
you reached for their hand
and found betrayal instead
that was the moment
the knife entered the story

the knife that glints
not just with blood
but with truth

not the truth
they tell you in sermons
but the kind that lives
beneath the fox's tongue
and behind the owl's eyes

the bones of your trust
cracked
the meat of your love
tore
and suddenly you
were pieces

not a whole

shattered belief
stared up at you
from the floor

and from those shards
a song began
one only the broken-hearted
can hear

betrayal is a teacher
with no bedside manner
it does not knock
it kicks the door in
it steals your name
tears your map
burns your house
and hands you a flint

now the forest waits
dark
unforgiving
holy
you walk it alone
barefoot
your silence
louder than drums

and yet
somewhere beyond
the wolf's howl
and the thorn's kiss
you begin to understand
the knife didn't just cut you
it carved you
it opened a place
where the old knowing
could enter

you are not the same
you are never the same
you wear your wound
like a resolution now
knowing one day it
will become a scar
a talisman
a testimony

not proud
but true

you learned to read tracks
by walking lost
you learned to hear truth
by choking on lies
you learned who you are
when they showed you
who they were not

and so
you rise

not despite the betrayal
but because of it

not hardened
not bitter
but sharpened
clear

a blade in your own hand now
not to harm
but to cut through illusion
to slice open the next story
and begin again

this time
awake

JAWBONE OF FORGIVENESS

forgiveness
is not a white flag
it is not a handshake
at a polished table
under the cold lights of compromise

it is the antler
left on your doorstep
by something wild
that has watched you
from the edge of the wood
for seasons too long to name

it is the beast
that stalks the perimeter dark
around your bitter burning
on paws of blood
and mercy
tufts of furred grace lodged
in its jawbone

forgiveness
is not forgetting
it is remembering
and still choosing
to lay the blade down
in the grass

it is the moment
you meet the ghost of the person
who broke you
and they do not bow
but you do

not in surrender

in understanding

because now you know
they were carrying
their own pile of savage stones
their own famine of love
and though it doesn't
excuse the wound
it explains the ruin

forgiveness
is the long walk home
after the avalanche
it is the breath you take
before digging down
to a story you buried
as the pain buried you

it is not tidy
it is not noble
it is the craggy voice
of the old woman in the mountain
who jabs at your bruise
with her message
the only way out
is through

forgiveness
is crawling on your knees
through the shards
of your own story
finding the child
you left behind
when the shattering
was at its loudest

it is holding her
not fixing her
not changing her
holding her
tenderly
imperfectly
while rocking her scorched
hummingbird body
and saying
*we made it
love—
we made it*

it is laying your pain
at the altar of the phoenix
inside your own soul

it is remembering yourself
indestructible

not forgetting the fire
but learning
how to carry its ember and ash
without setting
everything else
ablaze

PRIDE

god didn't whisper
when she made you
she sang
she exalted *let there be glitter*
and **you happened**

the stars leaned in
to hear her say
more sparkle
more shine
make their heart soft
and their spirit loud
make their walk
a runway
make their laugh
a hymn

she carved your curves
and sharp edges
out of moonlight
and confetti
she painted your pride
in every color
they tried to erase

you are
not a mistake
or a phase
or the footnote
in the story

you're the fireworks
you're the divine disco ball
twirling in the sanctuary
casting holy light
on everyone
who forgot how to dance

you are not too much
you are not wrong
you are a love letter
written in her own handwriting
festive and fabulous
and shiny on purpose

when you gaze at your life
let your chest fill
with royal pride
'cuz you were made
in her image
love pie—
and damn
she's a queen

THE SECOND FIRE

there is a rage
older than your name
it does not come from the mind
it rises from the marrow
from the salt caves of the ancestors
from the soil where bones remember
what was taken

this is not the rage that burns barns
for the sake of watching them collapse
no
this is *sacred* rage
the kind that stands
at the edge of the forest
and howls
because the trees can no longer speak

the kind that comes
when the lies grow too tall
when the pigs wear silk
when the grief has nowhere else to go

this is the rage that cups
a broken truth in both hands
and says *this is not how it ends*

sacred rage does not destroy
it *reveals*
it peels back the satin of civility
to show the holy heart beating
beneath the bruise
it is the lioness waking
in the cave of your belly
the heron screeching
in the glade of your chest
the storm that does not ask permission
to clear the air

this is the *second fire*
the first was made
to warm your hands
but this one is made
to heat your spine
to make your back remember
it was not born to bend

this rage speaks
in the old tongue
the language of drumbeat and dream
of mothers not believed
of forests flattened
of lovers buried in silence

it does not scream
it *names*
it does not burn bridges
it *builds altars*

so when the sacred rage comes
don't run
sit by its side
ask it what it knows
then rise
lit from within

ARC

you will stumble
you will fall
you will burn
but you will also
like the phoenix

fly

your wings are made
from every hand
that has lifted you
from the flames

and each hand
you offer to those
still trapped below

reach
forgive
fly

THE REACH

It happens.

One minute you're soaring. The next minute you're grounded. Your cheek hits the floor. Hard. You taste blood.

Just when you think it couldn't be worse, the trap door springs open. You freefall into the dark abyss.

Playing cautious won't save you. Trying to be perfect won't protect you. It's happening, and it's a gift. A dark, fucked-up painful gift that you probably won't see until long after it's over.

But in the middle of plunging and burning, new wings are formed. New life is forged. All that's old and worn-out burns away.

And in the dark, there are hands.

Hands made of music, poems, stories. Hands made of hugs, gestures, grace. Hands reaching for you, always reaching, to bring you back into sky.

Eventually, you're out. You're up. And you're not only flying; you're soaring. It's still you, but new. Wings formed from fire burn across the sky. There is no stopping you.

Until one day you hear the cries.

You ground yourself, willingly. You slow your wings and lean down to the ground, putting the ear of your soul against the trap door. You hear them. So you reach. Reach down your hands. The hands of your words. The hands of your stories. The hands of your poem, your art, your grace.

Those hands reach down, clasping others reaching up in an arc of hope and possibility. Your hands say: *Yes you can* and *Now is the time*. Your wings whisper: *The fire is not the end. It is a beginning.*

Now there are more of you. The clouds blur with the shape of resurrection.

There are wings, wings everywhere reaching up and hands, hands ever reaching back as the sky unfolds with the flight of belonging.

THE COST OF FORGETTING

when we teach them
that everything real
must be earned
that joy has a price tag
that love is conditional
that belonging must be begged for
we do not raise children
we raise ghosts
in living skin

we teach them to abandon
their own magic
at the gates of approval
to trade their wonder
for permission
to starve their wild
just to be fed
crumbs of acceptance

we make them apprentices
to a false god named *Deserving*
and we forget:
the moon does not ask
if you've worked hard enough
to see her
she simply shines
the wind does not check
your credentials
before it kisses your cheek
it just arrives
brave and uninvited

and oh the ache
when we pretend otherwise

when we pretend
the sacred must be earned
we lead them into a cage
too small for their dreaming
we close the door
on their lion-heart
and call it *discipline*

but your soul was never made
for small economies

your spirit does not bloom
on barter

you were born
to receive without proving
to speak without shrinking
to dance without debt

the flowers do not hustle
the mountains do not beg
the stars do not perform
they just *are*
and in their being
they bless us

so remember
when we tell someone
they must earn
what is already theirs
we are not guiding them
we are shrinking them
we are dressing their sacred
in shame

and the cost is this:
a world full of quiet grief
people half-alive
still waiting
for permission
to take a deep breath

but not you

you remember now
you feel it stirring
that wildness
that truth

you were never meant
to be good

you were meant
to be *whole*

FAITH

The shattering is jagged, personal and entirely too intimate, like rape. Like a thief stealing away the last bloom of hope from your garden of belief.

That's what I'm thinking as I walk down the tiny one-track lane flanked by low, grey, stack-stone walls on a tiny Irish island.

When betrayal happens, when a cherished someone violates your trust and boundaries, the pain eviscerates all belief. Which is both dangerous and deadly for someone whose life is shaped by her belief in things invisible.

The pain cuts from the inside. I can hardly breathe. Each inhale feels serrated. Each exhale feels wet and suffocating. This is nothing new. I've been through this too many times. Which tempts me towards shame, and self-blame. I'm losing my faith in relationships. In family. Life. Myself.

I'm in danger. Not because my mind can't conceive that *this too shall pass,* but because I'm tired—soul tired. World weary. In blood, bones, pulse. I've gone past what my human form feels it can endure. My soul is on suicide watch for my heart. For my life. It tries to barricade the exit doors as I consider leaving the planet.

I hear the *clop-clop* of horse hooves and move out of the lane, up against the stacked stones, to make way for the pony trap. That's when I see it.

Shoved between the flat stones of the wall, a little piece of sunshine. Is it a peach? A stray Easter egg abandoned by a forgetful bunny?

It's neither. It's faith. A palm-sized, pastel-painted smooth rock with the word *FAITH* in block letters.

Faith is a stranger I once knew intimately. We parted ways when I escaped organized religion, having survived years in the IFB cult. I witnessed too many atrocities perpetrated in its name—*people of faith* encouraging eyes and hearts skyward while their sticky fingers and dirty hands violated.

I survived and retained my relationship with love. With grace and forgiveness and compassion. But I ditched faith at a small bar outside of Houston. While Fleetwood Mac was playing on the jukebox, I slipped out the bathroom window in search of more accountable words like resonance, truth, integrity. Today I still connect to the concept of "evidence of things unseen," but I experience it more like oxygen. Just because you don't see it and aren't aware of it, doesn't mean it's not there, working on your behalf.

So this rock with its chipped faith appearing to me now? With its pastel shock of cotton-candy encouragement? It quickens something in me. Not in a bearded-god-in-the-sky kind of way, or a heavens-parting-with-cherubs kind of way. It's more of a my-guardian-angel-drinks kind of way. Clearly, he stumbled home from the pub last night and, having tumbled into the wall while taking a wee, decided to remind me of unseen allies with a rock-shaped Post-it note. My guardian angel swaggers a lot like David Tennant in *Good Omens*.

Invisibles is the word I most often use to describe the beings who look out for me. It's them I sense, standing there in the middle of the road. *We are still here. I seem to hear them say. No matter what's going on in your current circumstances, we are available. We are the reality beyond your illusion. Use us.*

So I put the rock in my jacket and walk to the singular pub in town for lunch. It feels heavy, weighing down my pocket with a dangerous light. I prop it on the table, against the breadbasket, next to the pint of Orchard Thieves Wild cider. The glass has a fox on it, ready to steal an apple from a garden. I watch the tiny golden bubbles moving skyward, wondering if I'm going to have to break into my own orchard of pain to steal back some faith. I hear the words of my teachers in my head: *This isn't happening to you. It's happening for you.*

That's a shitty message to consider when you're shattered. Don't ever tell a broken heart that message while it's still trying to regain its rhythm. But damn if it doesn't contain resonance, truth, integrity. Damn if I don't drink from that cup's message and feel the bubbles rising. Damn if the shattered begins to feel ... something. That's all, just something. Upward.

This is not the part where I tell you the clouds parted, the angels sang, and every healing possibility came into focus. It's not the part where I tell you my energy and heart were suddenly restored. It's the part where I tell you I could take a breath. That's it. Just one breath that didn't feel like choking on glass. And that, too, was something.

I drank down the stolen-apple bubbles, ate my chicken salad, returned the rock to my pocket and walked back to my lodging. The sound of the sea was in my ears. Somewhere, a distant seal was barking. Somewhere, a donkey was braying. The world would continue its daily spin as my grief-laden pockets jumbled to make room for their new roommate, faith.

I didn't walk the forests or climb the cliffs or join the selkies on the beach. I crawled into bed with my book, then climbed back out to get that damn rock. Book in one hand, faith in the other, I read and cried all night. Then did it again the next day. Many days.

When you trust the wrong people, whether they be lover, family, friend or government, the shatter overtakes you. Violation grabs you in its death grip. You, too, have hands. You get to choose what you hold onto. Sometimes all you've got is the invisible. And sometimes that's enough.

Just one inhale at a time curled into the fetal position. One story. One nap. One song. One rock or poem or furry bestie cuddle. No one gets to tell you what your resilience looks like. Or your grief. But the invisibles can tell you what your soul looks like, and that's rock solid. Reliable. Available.

And ever
always
only
upwards.

THE ACHE
THAT KNOWS YOUR NAME

there is a kind of longing
that doesn't want an answer
it wants the wind
through the pines
at dusk
wants the sound of antlers
clashing somewhere
deep in the bracken
of your own chest
it wants the thing
you cannot name
but feel
like a ghost hand
on your shoulder
just before sleep

longing
real longing
is not for comfort
it is a wild animal
circling the fire
watching you forget
that you too
have teeth

you were not made
to be satisfied
you were made
to be torn open
by beauty
too fierce to hold

there is holiness
in the hunger
that does not end
it's how the soul
remembers
what the body forgot
the path
the story
the place in the forest
where your name
was first spoken
by the earth

so let it ache
let the longing
build its nest
in your ribs

one day
it may become
a pair of wings

A LETTER FOR EEYORE

dear Eeyore,

I know
sometimes the sky
stays gray
even when the sun
says hello
and the thistle tastes bitter
and your tail won't stay on
and everything feels
like a long slow trudge
through mud-soaked Mondays

but listen
I love you anyway

I love you
even when your head hangs low
and your voice is made of sighs
even when you think
you're too much
or not enough
or something in between

you don't have to be cheerful
to be cherished
you don't have to bounce
or whistle
or shine

you just have to be here
exactly as you are
a little droopy
a little blue
but always
always
worthy of love

and if you forget
I'll remind you

I'll remind you
with quiet things
cozy blankets
and warm tea
and sitting beside you
when you can't find your way
back to happy

the Hundred Acre Wood
wouldn't be the same
without your footsteps
even if they are slow

so rest Eeyore
I'm not going anywhere

love,
me

WINGS

this tightness in your chest
this ache in your bones
they're not signs
of failure or fatigue
you're outgrowing
your old shape

a robin inside a shell
a butterfly in a cocoon
a fire dragon inside
a scaled egg
a woman in a life
that no longer fits

wings
are notorious
for growing
in tight places

STORYTELLER

they keep asking you to be resilient
to bend without breaking
to return to your original shape
after being scorched by fire

but you were never meant
to become the shape
they made of you

you are not rubber
you are not brick
you are not fortress or wall
you are wild soil
you are loam
dreaming itself into lichen
a song seeded in ash
that hums green under the ribs

resilience says
endure the storm
regeneration says
marry it

go barefoot into the downpour
and let it court you
let the rain have your tongue
let the grief soak you through
until mushrooms bloom
where your sorrow once slept

this is not about bouncing back
this is about breaking open
like pomegranate skin
so the seeds of your own myth
can take root in the dark

let the wolves smell your becoming
let the roots stitch your name
into the underworld
let the nettles teach you
how to sting and soften
in the same breath

because surviving the story
is not the same
as becoming the storyteller

you are not a monument
to suffering well
you are a forest
in the making
feral
flowering
and gloriously undone

STAY IN YOUR STARLIGHT

every time you lace up your boots
and march into someone else's wilderness
thinking you know better
which path they should take
which tree they should climb
which direction they should walk
you lose your way back home

you think it's love
you call it care
but love
true love
the kind with wings and roots
never grabs the compass
from trembling hands

love waits at the crossroads
with warm tea
and a lantern
it doesn't plot shortcuts
for someone else's journey

because every time
you try to control their path
you step off your own
that starlit
serpentine
wildflower-slicked path
the one carved
by your own tears
and tantrums and triumphs

you were not born
to be a shepherd
for every lost soul
that calls your name
you were born
to set fires from your belly
and sing maps from your bones

so let them walk
let them stumble
let them curse the sky
and fall in love with it anyway
your job
is not to save them
your job
is to shine
so fiercely
so truthfully
that they remember
they are made of light too

stay in your starlight
love pie—
because the moment
you trade your fire
for their flashlight
you go dark
and they go blind

BRILLIANTLY BAD

this is your permission slip to fail
signed by stardust
notarized by moonlight
delivered by the misfit angels
who color outside every line

yes
you

with the trembling hands
and the brave heart
that's pretending not to pound
you're allowed
to mess it all up

paint the picture
that looks like chaos
write the poem
that doesn't rhyme
try the dance with two left feet
with joy as your only rhythm

you don't need to be perfect
to be precious
this world was not built
by those who got it right
on the first try
it was stitched together by souls
who dared to fall
dared to rise
dared to laugh
with ashes on their nose
and failure at their feet

start the thing
wreck it
begin again

you're not behind
you're becoming

looking foolish
is the costume of the brave

so go ahead
be gloriously brilliantly
bad at it
that's where the gold lives
not in the polish
but in the play

this is your permission slip
to fail
and in doing so
to fly

THE WAY

Etched into the surface of the silver band on my wrist this morning are words from an 800-year-old prophet. I found the bracelet on a trip to Northern California not long after I retaught my body to walk following a nightmarish spinal surgery that rendered me paralyzed from the neck down. This was my victory trip.

I was 29 years old. On the outside. Inside life had inverted me. I felt 92. Trauma can do that to you.

With all the terrifying news headlines of late, you feel as though you've aged overnight. Your heart may be graying at the temples. Your hope groaning and stiff when it tries to rise. The knees of your forgiveness may creak when you attempt to pray for better, for equal, for fair.

These words by Rumi encircle my wrist, but I can feel them reaching towards my heart as my pen reaches towards yours:

Drum beat rises on the air.
It's throb, my heart.
A voice inside the beat says
I know you are tired.
But come.
This is the way.

When you can no longer hear the melody of life, listen to the rhythm. When the rhythm fades, cling to the beat. Come back to the drum right there in your chest. Part lullaby, part battle cry, it is a map.

Ever beating, not beaten.

This is the way.

A SPELL FOR WHEN YOU FEEL LIKE LEAVING

darling love pie—
I see you
shoulders sagging under
a sky that won't speak
hope leaking from the edges
of yesterday's dreams

today
love feels like a mountain
you weren't built to climb
like the tea has gone cold
like your hands forgot
how to hold light
so here
take this spell
tuck it behind your ear
like wildflower secrets

let it root

may you remember:
you are not required
to bloom every morning
you are allowed
to be seed
to be soil
to be still

may you know:
love is not only
the grand gesture
the falling star
the kiss that turns the tide
sometimes
love is just
getting out of bed
with a tired heart
and brushing your teeth
like an act of rebellion

sometimes
love is not running
when it all goes quiet
not shutting down
when it gets too loud

may you trust:
your softness is armor
your ache is proof
you're still open
you still care
you still believe
in beautiful things
even if you've forgotten
how to say so out loud

may you dare:
to stay
to sip your tea slowly
to water the wilted places
to tell the shadows
not today
to choose the tiniest spark
and call it holy

this is not the end
this is a pause
a sacred exhale
in the symphony
of becoming

so light your candle
speak your name
like it's a prayer
wrap your arms
around your own ribs
and whisper
I am not broken
I am becoming
and that
is more than enough

FRACTURE

your soul is Xanadu
heart full of roller skates
veins full of glitter

don't be dismayed
by the fractured world
attempting to break
your light

apart

a disco ball is
splintered glass

spackled together
to make a sparkly ball
of magic light

you aren't broken

you're a disco ball

and the world is
your dance floor

STILL

life hurt me
left me in the cold
with a broken compass
and promises that cracked
like cheap porcelain

she told me
to dream big
then swallowed those dreams
whole
like some kind of hungry goddess

she's stolen from me
smashed me into splinters
watched me beg the stars
for a different ending

and still
I love her

not because she is gentle
but because she is real
because in the same hands
that tore me down
she offered
a warm cup of wind
a laughing fox
a sunrise
that didn't need to explain itself

because just when I think
I can't take another step
life sends me
a song
a stranger
a storm that clears the air

she shows me
that even ruin
can bloom
that joy
doesn't wait
for perfection

she dances
right into the mess
and throws glitter
on the floor

yes life is sharp
she bites
she forgets birthdays
she sometimes feels
like betrayal
dressed up in fairy lights
but she is also
the reason
I keep opening my heart
like a cathedral
even when the stained glass
has shattered again

because love like this
love that knows the cost
is no longer fragile
it's holy
it's fire-breathing
it's mine

so no
I do not trust her to be kind
but I trust myself
to meet her
with courage
again and again
heart cracked wide
and arms outstretched
whispering
still
still
I choose you

PROMISES KEPT

you made a promise
like a ribbon in the wind
bright
beautiful
and never meant to hold

you said *forever*
with a voice that tasted
of honey in summer
but turned to ash
in winter's mouth

here's what you didn't know
I believed you
not because I was weak
but because I was wild
because I still thought
promises were spells
that meant something

and when you broke them
not all at once
but slowly
like petals dropping
from a dying bloom
something ancient
stirred in me

it wasn't sorrow
though I wept
it wasn't rage
though I burned
it was older than both

it was bone memory
wolf wisdom
the sound of claws
unsheathing in the dark
your lies fed something
hungry in me
your silence
taught me to sing
to the moon
instead of you
your vanishing act
showed me
my own reflection
in the river
alone yes
but powerful
untamed

and oh—
the claws

they weren't born
of vengeance
but of truth
they grew in the place
where I clutched
every sorry you never said

now I do not beg
I do not shrink
I do not wait for a door
that swings only one way
I speak storm and gale
I walk with bear
I listen like stars
and kiss with spider fire
on my tongue

you gave me nothing
but empty vows
and still
I made a
feral kingdom

you made a promise
like a ribbon in the wind
bright
beautiful
and never meant to hold

I tied that ribbon
on my finger
as reminder and resolve
to always use the gift
your emptiness gave me

claws like promises kept

DAFFODILS AND STARDUST

when the world cracked open
when sirens screamed louder
than lullabies
when headlines broke
like glass
and the air trembled
with fear
you reached
not for the sword
but for the shimmer

you reached for wonder

they said
this is not the time for dreaming
but your bones knew better
your blood had danced
with too many moons
to forget
it is always time for dreaming

you lit candles
not just for light
but to remember magic
you stirred honey
into your tea
and whispered gratitude
to the bees
you wore feathers
in your hair
and painted your lips
the color of rebellion

you laughed
full-bodied and belly-deep
the kind that makes tyrants
uneasy

and when the sky fell
you didn't flinch
you spun yourself
a cloak of daffodils and stardust
and faced it
barefoot
wild-eyed
feral
divine

because wonder
true wonder
is not naïve
it is not soft
it is not the fragile thing
they told you it was

it is forged
in the furnace
of sorrow
tempered by tears
shaped by gratitude
blessed by scorched earth
and scalding forgiveness

it is the shield you carry
when the world forgets
how to be kind

it is the spell you cast
when the news bites too hard

it is how you remember
that you are more
than just a survivor

you are a seer
a sorceress
a keeper of stars
who remembers
it takes the dark
to know yourself
as the light

BIGGER ON THE INSIDE

You know that stellar moment when Harry Potter enters the Weasley's small, drab tent only to discover it's a huge, multi-roomed, colorful splendor inside? Magic, my friend. *Magic.*

Wanna know how to create that in your own life? It's available without ever stepping foot inside Hogwarts. It doesn't require a wizard, a wand or a spell. But it does require the magic of forgiveness.

Every time you forgive someone their fuckery (even when they didn't ask), every time you extend grace, every time you let go of a betrayal, every time you forgive yourself for falling or failing or letting yourself down, you become bigger on the inside.

Because grace is like helium: it expands and uplifts. It's a kind of magic. But not everyone can wield that wizardry. We often think that things must be *right* before they're *okay.* Not true. Things can be incredibly, horribly wrong and you can still be okay. Because when we let go, we are demonstrating that we care more about our own well-being than we care about being right, or having the situation conform to our version of justice.

When we accept the apology that never came and forgive someone who never asked, we rise. When we forgive ourselves and expand into our own vast potential, we add another room to our soul home. It's not easy. It's not clean or clear cut. But it is simple. You decide that your worth is determined by you alone.

Glossy social media would have you chasing after an 8-bedroom mansion in Beverly Hills with a gilded staircase and a six-car garage. Fuck that. I'll take my brightly-woven-genie-bottle-ever-expanding-made-of-miracles tent. It fits in my backpack. It's lighter than a spell book. And there's an entire room made of balloons. I keep my unicorn in there.

He's bigger on the inside, too.

RAINBOW

you are not your chaos
your crisis
your pain
you are not your mistakes
your brokenness
your regret
you are not your past
your wounds or
even your survival

you are the result
of all these things
unfolding in the
ever-present now

choosing again
choosing anew

to remember your divine origins
to claim the multi-dimensional
magnificence
of your soul
right in the middle
of the chaos

you are not the survivor
of the storm

you are the storm

and the wild blue sea
and the calm of waves
lapping the shore
when all is said and done

and the rainbow
you are the fucking rainbow

promising every hopeful heart
that gazes at your radiance
this too shall pass

THE POP QUIZ

let's be honest
love pie—
make everyday count
sounds like something a mug says
right before you spill coffee
all over your to-do list

there are days
when all you can count
is how many crumbs
are in your bra
or how many times
you've forgotten
why you walked into the kitchen

that's okay
that counts too

some mornings
you open your eyes
and the world feels
like a pop quiz
you didn't study for

but here's the cheat sheet:
you don't have to earn your place
on the spinning globe
breathing is enough today
feeding the cat is enough
saying *I'm trying*
counts for more than you think

love isn't tracking
how many vegetables you eat
or whether your inbox is tamed
she's likely curled up
on your unmade bed
murmuring
rest beloved
you're not a machine

so skip the pressure-cooker life plan
let the minutes be messy
let the moments be small
eat cheese toast for dinner
call it a win

you showed up
you were here

make every day *mean* something?
sure
but sometimes
just surviving it
is meaning enough

WHY REJECTION IS RAD

Empaths. Romantics. Dreamers. We are sometimes over-givers, people-pleasers, doormats. We are willing to go great distances for love. Marathons even. Uphill. In the snow. Often for the unwilling or the ungrateful.

The problem isn't them. Their unwillingness to see you, appreciate you, give back to you or even meet you halfway? It's their way of nudging you in the direction of your people. And your acceptance? Your ability to let them be who they are without judging them for not loving you or not including you, or not giving back to you what you need? It's your way of making space for your people.

Their rejection is a favor.

It's having one of those awesome maps with the red dot that says YOU ARE HERE. Only rejection? It's a black arrow that says YOU ARE NOT HERE. This isn't for you. No matter how good you think it is. No matter how perfect for you he seems, or how amazingly that job would suit your needs, or how that one thing would help you be the person you just know deep down you can be.

YOU ARE NOT HERE, says the big black arrow of rejection.

Your place, your people, are elsewhere. That big arrow is pointing you away.

And when we stop taking that personally, when we stop interpreting that as a judgement on how pretty or smart or worthwhile we are, when we stop thinking it means we are less valuable or loveable, when we stop making the rejection our whole story and our life's worth, then we can say *thank you*.

Thank you for showing me where I don't belong. I'm one step closer to finding out where I do.

Thank you for showing me where not to spend my time and energy, so I don't live life constantly feeling depleted and not good enough.

Thank you for leading me towards what makes me radiant rather than desperate.

Thanks for encouraging me to find the value inside my heart instead of inside another.

Thanks, rejection!

All the right people will reject you to make room for all the right people to accept you.

And if you're in a job or a relationship or situation that feels like work, feels uphill, feels desperate or anxious or rejecting? You're in the wrong place.

The rejection is shouting YOU ARE NOT HERE.

Your essence, your connection, your love is elsewhere.

Go find it.

When rejection has nudged and pushed and shoved you away from what you're not, and you're standing on the map, right at the little red dot of mutuality and appreciation, with a heart that announces YOU ARE HERE, you're gonna smile about all the bitter, resentful losses and sigh: *Thanks rejection. You're freakin' rad.*

THE SHACKLES

you give them
the last match from your fire
you pour your heart rain
into their drought
you hand them roadmaps
out of their confusion
only to find the directions wadded up
on the floorboards
of their dismissal

no matter how many keys
you offer
they stay in the dungeon
with the door wide open
clutching their shackles
like family heirlooms

you try to be a lighthouse
but they keep stalking rocks
and smashing boats

this is how you learn
the hard holy
inconvenient truth

you are not the architect
of anyone else's awakening

you may light a torch
sing a song
offer a prayer
unlatch the gate
but the walking?
that's not yours

love fiercely
offer fully
but don't burn
down your temple
to keep someone else warm

you have to meet people
where they are
and sometimes
for the sake of sanity
and sovereignty
you have to leave them there

BLACK SHEEP GOSPEL

they named you black sheep
like it was a curse
like it wasn't a crown
woven from wildness
and the willingness
to see
what they spend lifetimes
pretending not to

they said you were difficult
when you dared to speak the words
that cracked the family's porcelain smile
you asked the questions
that made the silence flinch
unwrapped the gifts buried beneath
the generational hush-hush

you
beloved—
are not broken
you are *breaking*
the cycles
the lies
the lineage
of smallness
you are the storm that baptizes
not destroys

while they cling
to heirlooms of denial
you carry medicine
bittersweet and holy
you name the shadows
so they can no longer rule
you tell the truth
with your whole throat
even when it shakes
especially when it shakes

and yes
you have been exiled
eye-rolled
edited from the holiday photo
but you are not lost
you are *forged*
by fire
by freedom
by the ache of authenticity

you are the healer in exile
the prophet in boots
tracking ancestral ghosts
through the underbrush
singing lullabies to the child inside
who only ever wanted to be seen
not as scapegoat
but as sacred

this is your altar
this is your rite
to speak
to shatter
to shine

because the black sheep
was never the villain
only the first to wake up
while everyone else
was dreaming of perfection

and the flock may never follow
but oh how the world needs
your wild gospel

carry on
you beautiful
truth-telling
chain-breaking
miracle

WHAT IT MEANS TO FLY

fail splendidly
fall spectacularly
fuck
it up
mercilessly

I am less interested
in your successes
and more interested
in the ravenous heart
that led you
one more time
to get back up

again

sweaty and
smelly and laughing
at your own
brilliant
fractured
humanity

flailing
and failing
but flying
oh yes
my dear—
flying

look at you go

THE WHIP

forgiving yourself
might not feel heroic

no cape
no trumpet
just dishes in the sink
and a heart
that finally exhaled

but trust me

letting go
of the whip in your hand
is the bravest damn thing
you'll ever do

JUICY MESSY GORGEOUS

tenderness isn't weakness
or softness
it's the most powerful thing
you can offer yourself
and others

to throw your arms
fiercely
around your lost
broken places
and nod tenderly
at all the screaming want
the mistakes
the wrong turns

sitting side by side
with grace
as you remember yourself
back to found
that is real power

inconvenient feelings
are an invitation
for you to meet
the real you
the juicy you
the messy gorgeous you
living in the world
of clean convenience

but dying to get out
dying to get real
dying to live
the sparkle
that comes
from healed
fracture

don't cower when
life grows dim
don't hide in the shade
and grow small

your heart is the moon

rise in
the
darkness

and shine

THE RIDE

darling love pie—
the world is mad with motion
a carnival ride where no one checked
the bolts or the brakes
and you are trying
to sip tea in a hurricane
like it's just another Tuesday

I see you
gripping grace like a lifeline
tying hope like ribbons
around your bruised heart
clutching your courage
like a war-torn teddy bear

this is how you feel safe
in an unsafe world
you build altars
out of absurdity
you wear glitter
to the grocery store
you sing to the moon
like she's your backup therapist
and maybe she is

you collect joy like firewood
even the damp kind
even the splinters
because winter comes
and you'll need the warmth

you stop expecting
the world to be gentle
and start insisting
that you will be

not because you're naïve
oh no
because you're a storm witch
in pearls
because you've learned
that softness is a rebellion
that kindness is a lacy dagger
that cuts the jagged edge
of hatred

you pull your safety
from within
you brew tea with invisibles
and tell them stories
of your becoming

you wear your scars
like a secret map
and bless the ache
that taught you how to rise

you feel safe
not because the world is safe
but because you made
a cathedral in your ribcage
a cradle in your heart
a candle behind the windowsill
of your eyes

and when the chaos howls
you dance anyway
you love anyway
you live anyway
because you
love pie—
have magic in your marrow
and the storm
has nothing on a woman
who makes a sanctuary
out of herself

JULY

true independence
isn't a parade
it's not fireworks cracking
above strip malls
or boozy barbeque grills
in backyards
it's not flags on t-shirts
made in factories far away
by hands that never got to vote

it's smaller than that
quieter
holier
it's the decision
to wake up
when despair
wants you to stay down
to feed the dog
to water the plant
that hasn't bloomed in weeks
but still
reaches for the light
like it believes
something's coming

it's laughing
when the news says not to
crying without apologizing
having your neighbor's back
when the laws say
we're meant to be strangers

true independence
is lighting a candle
while the world burns
not because it will save us
but because
you promised your soul
you wouldn't forget
how to glow

it's yelling into the void
and then writing
a poem about it
it's calling your senator
and then baking
chocolate chip cookies
with too many chips
because we're still here
and sweetness still matters

it's not freedom
in the way they package it
shiny
privileged
weaponized

it's freedom
in the way grace works
unruly
defiant
always showing up
with bad hair
and open arms

true independence is this:
you still care
you still love
you still believe
in a better country
even if it hasn't arrived yet
even if it's just
you and a friend
and a cup of coffee
and the raw furious prayer
that says
we will not give up
on each other

not now
not ever

TRUE WEALTH

allow me to harsh
your mellow
by revealing what you've
been hiding
from yourself

that bundle of anxiety
is not a life
it's a prison sentence
and the only way to
unfuck yourself
is straight through soul

use it as a prism
to glimpse the real you
the infinite oceanic sparkle
of you

'cuz you're not the pearl
inside the oyster
you're not even the oyster
you're the whole freakin' ocean
and your soul is littered
with pirate treasure
and mermaid taverns

you're a vast sea
of unimaginable wealth

get out there
and spend it

WAR PAINT

they told me
wonder
was a childish thing
something to tuck away
with the dolls and dreams
but
I kept it anyway
hidden
in my ribcage
like a forbidden star

I watered it
with tears
fed it
moonlight
sang lullabies
when the world
got too loud
and now
it blooms
in the cracks
where life
tried to break me

call me foolish
call me soft
call me whatever
makes you feel safe
or superior
but know this:

my wonder
is not weak
it has survived
every shame invasion
every battle against despair
it is the strongest
part of me

and we will not
go quietly

ORIGAMI IMAGINATION

when it comes to the
tattered storybook
of our fractured world
and your own
brokenness too
do yourself a favor

use that sparkly
unicorn brain of yours
to create something new

fold your paperback tears
into origami dreams
and give them flight

shape the wounds
into wings
and send them
into a future
feathered with hope

stop imagining
the apocalypse
and start imagining
the revolution

FERAL HOPE

hope is not
a porcelain swan
balanced on a shelf
waiting for gentle hands

no
love pie—
hope is a streetfighter
with split lips
and fists full of thunder

she's got blood on her face
dirt under her nails
gravel in her teeth
and a laugh that echoes
like war drums
through the bones of despair

she's not delicate
she's defiant

she doesn't wear white
she wears smoke and fire
draped in the armor of all the times
she should've stayed down
but didn't

you'll find her in the ring
long after the bell's been rung
shoulder to shoulder
with heartbreak
eye to eye with doubt
smiling that sideways grin
that says
try me again

this is not greeting card hope
not pastel-painted sweet-toothed hope
this is feral hope
mud-streaked and battle-born
the kind that howls prayers
into storm clouds
and makes them open

she's the one
who shows up
when your knees buckle
and the world goes dark
not to rescue you
but to remind you
you're made of the same stuff

so rise
beloved

rise with the dirt
rise with the scars
rise with hope
that looks a lot like you
scraped up
lit up
and ready
for another round

JANUARY

you are a revolution
not a resolution
instead of making resolutions to fix
your beautifully imperfect life
spend January making lists
of all the reasons
your life is already awesome

you have a heart that feels
deeply

you have a great sense of humor
your laugh is awesome
your smile changes a room
there is a tenderness
and a fierceness
that live inside your chest
and they can create
a revolution

let that revolution
be your own belonging

sing for no reason
skip to your car in the parking lot
when you feel down give yourself a hug
and treat yourself the way you would
an injured deer on the side of the road
find a jukebox and dance
lay down on a patch of grass and
let the earth talk to you
listen hard

float
sparkle
giggle 'til you snort
use more jazz hands
show someone your butt
not because it's perfect
but because you have one
and it deserves to be
adored

you'll always find proof
of what you look for
so stop seeking what's wrong
with the world
what's wrong with you
how life has shortchanged you
or how you don't fit in

start seeking the proof
of your belonging

a prophet once said
love is the whole
and we are the pieces

start acting like it

you fit right here
with me
with us
with love

sparkle on
you gorgeous fucking thing

MAMA BEAR

they left you
at the doorstep
of their small love

told you
that you were
too much
too soft
too queer
too you
for the brittle box
they built from fear

they slammed doors
with bible verses
and bruised your name
with shame
but hear me now
love pie—
you didn't lose a family
you lost a cage
and I?
I've been waiting
with wide arms
and wilder hair
in a kitchen that smells
like magic and cookies
and something ancient that says
you belong

come in
kick off those
battle-weary boots
this den is for you
this love?
it doesn't expire
it doesn't come with
cramped conditions
it doesn't ask you to shrink
or shape-shift
into someone less complex

it says *yes*
exactly as you are
yes
full
fucking
stop

because baby—
I've got enough love
to rebuild galaxies
and I've stitched a nebula
just for you
inside this hug

let them go
let me hold you
mama bear is on the scene
I've got claws sharp enough
to tear shame to ribbons
and fur soft enough
to catch every falling tear

I've got paws
that dance with river stars
a tongue that praises
honeycomb truth
and teeth that can bite back
any voice that claims
you're not enough

the rooms of my heart
are rainbow-built
you can move in anytime
what you doing later today?
'cuz if that family of origin
can't accommodate
a bonafide miracle
their time is over

tick tock tick tock
it's miracle o'clock
BAM! BAM! SHAZAM!
I'm your family now

SHARK TEETH

they weren't expecting
the Care Bear
to grow shark teeth
but she did

after too many
midnight rescues
and people who took
her light
like it was free refills
at an all-night diner

after too many
you're too sensitive
and
can't you just be nice?
she snapped

but not the way they feared
not angry
not loud
not cruel

she just got
clear

she sewed boundaries
into her pelt
like secret seams

stitched *no*
into the hem
of her *yes*

she learned that
you can't keep shining
if you let every hand
reach in
to rearrange your stars

and the shark teeth?
they're not for biting
they're for guarding
the soft gold heart
that pumps out
every beam of love she gives

because real love
the kind that wakes the dead
and holds space for tears
and dances in moonlight
barefoot and howling
it doesn't survive
on martyrdom
it survives
on fierce
hell-no-yes-only-if-you-see-me
boundaries

so now
she hugs with her whole soul
but only if you come
clean
kind
and willing
to bring your own light
to the table

the Care Bear
still cares
she just stopped bleeding
for people
who only came
to steal the color
from her rainbow

MORE

when they tell you
to settle down
that your heart is woven
of too much magic
and your ruby emerald
butterfly dreams
must fold up and go
back into the dark chrysalis

remember your wings
belong to the sky
wild wide and free
urging you to soar
and always settle for more

more laughter more faith
more joy more grace
more wings
where
there
were
wounds

SPARKLE

you told me
I was too much
too bright
too wild
too glitter-drunk on dreams

you tried to shrink me
to fit your grey little box
lined with rules
and silent submission

you said
don't shine so loud
don't laugh so big
don't wear your heart like confetti

but darling—
this light wasn't made
for dimmer switches
I was made
of stardust
and stage lights
fairy wings
and fire escapes
drenched in sequins
witch-fire and glimmer spells

you mistook
my radiance
for rebellion
when really
it was resurrection

I danced out
of your shadow
in heels
that sparked lightning
painted my mouth
with crimson rebellion
and wore my truth
like diamonds
you couldn't afford
to swallow

and now
you sit
on your cardboard throne
still preaching
that quiet is holy
and loud women
are dangerous

you're right
I am dangerous

I'm dangerous
to cages
to shame
to small gods
with big egos

so someday
when the light
you tried to kill
comes singing
down the street
in a parade of glitter gals
in voodoo boots
and war-painted laughter
it doesn't matter to me
whether you recognize
the girl you tried to
muzzle

but I hope
you choke a little bit
on all that sparkle

TACOS

here's the thing
no one tells you
until your mascara's half-cried off
and you're knee-deep
in peanut butter cups
wondering if anyone
has ever actually survived
being human:

you don't heal
by pretending it didn't happen
you don't grow
by faking serenity
you certainly don't evolve
by out-optimisming
the dumpster fire

you get better
by sitting down
next to the thing
you swore you'd never touch
the grief
the shame
the blistered ache
you carry from being
alive and awake
in this world
with a soft heart
and armor made of empathy

you scooch over
on the picnic bench
or the bar stool
and let the worst parts of you
sit down
you offer them a cup of tea
you don't fix them
you don't sage them
you just say:
well hell I guess we're in this together

and somehow
by the grace of mismatched socks
and second chances
the ache starts to breathe
the jagged bits
don't jab so hard
you remember
you've always been a little holy
and a lot stubborn
a little feral
and sometimes kind
and maybe that's enough

radical acceptance isn't sexy
it's not an Instagram filter
it's more like hugging a porcupine
because it's lonely
and so are you

but it's the doorway
it's the cracked-open window
where Love sneaks in
with a bag of tacos
and says
let's start here

THE LANTERN BEHIND YOUR RIBS

faith in dark times
is not a hymn
it is not sanctioned incense
in swinging braziers
it does not speak Latin
or wear white robes

faith in dark times
is the hand that keeps reaching
even when nothing
reaches back
it is the one ember
hidden under a decade of ash
that still dares to glow

it is not certainty
it is not clean answers
it is mud under your fingernails
and the scorch in your lungs
as you dig your way out

faith in dark times
is an injured thing
that limps beside you
that sleeps in your shadow
that growls when you try to quit

it will not save you
it will not spare you
but it will lope at the feet
of your dreams
and lick at the heels
of your hope
and whisper
we've been here before

as everything else falls away
you'll remember

the marrow of you
will hum with the knowledge
that the old stories were always
carried in the dark
not to escape it
but to conjure light
inside the gloom

to make a fire
in the belly of the whale
to find the stars
from the bottom of the well
to walk the underworld
with nothing but your breath
and a song

and that

that
is faith

not that it will be easy
not that you will be spared
but that your soul is older
than the storm

and the lantern
behind your ribs
still burns
still burns
still burns

ABOUT THE AUTHOR

Hi. I'm Angi. Thanks for buying my book. Or maybe someone gifted it to you, so thanks for reading my book. Maybe you haven't read it but just thumbed through it, so thank you for holding my book and making it feel special. No matter what you're doing with the book, you've landed on this page where I tell you that you are worthy of even more goodness than what I've been able to wrangle onto these pages.

I refer to my own brand of inspiration as muse juice, so if you're looking for a longer drink of that yumminess, please sign up on **angisullins.com**. This is where I notify my tribe of opportunities for online gatherings, workshops, world tours and oddball shenanigans.

Speaking of tribe, mine is called the Red Tent Blanket Fort. We meet on **facebook.com/AngiTv** where I post an original poem or essay every morning at 8am EST. Come in. Get cozy. Meet your tribe and fellow misfits. We delight in belonging to each other and to ourselves. Come for the poems, stay for the snacks.

Need more stardust in your teacup? Giving and receiving are intricately connected, so consider becoming one of my WonderHunters over on **patreon.com/angisullins**. This group of folks helps to keep my cup caffeinated and my pen drenched in inky goodness. You can also join for free, so don't let any constraint keep you from indulging.

I'm a poet priestess and have always wanted my own temple. Consider this an invocation to join my vision of one day meeting in our own space to break bread, share cookies and sip muse juice together. It's gonna happen.